On Your Own 101

101

Things You Forgot or Were Never Taught

• • •

A How-To Guide for

Real Life Scenarios

Copyright © 2011

Chris Kelly

Cover Design/Photos - Sara Sheridan

Developmental Editor – Shannon Evans

Copy Editor – Jennifer A. Evans

ISBN: 1453632808 and 9781453632802

Library of Congress Control Number Application Made

Dedication

I can't express enough of my deepest gratitude to my friends and family, who have always supported my endeavors and have pushed me when I needed it. I must especially thank my editor and fellow author, Shannon Evans for keeping her foot in my behind to get it done and then working out the kinks. Also, to my dear friend, Lotus Halligan, who gave me the title of this book. Terrence Kimble, thank you for showing my son Alexander how to clean the bathroom and patiently explaining why the bathroom should always be clean when you live on your own; this was my inspiration for the book. To my boys, Alexander and Asa Rabin for not letting on what their Mom is up to now. To my darling angel daughter, Theresa for bringing new joy to my life at the age of 44, who knew that mothering a daughter was so uniquely special. Finally, to Janet Pauli many thanks for being my number one fan.

I love you all! Let the new life begin!

On Your Own 101

Things You Forgot or Were Never Taught

A How To Guide For Real Life Scenarios

By Chris Kelly

Table of Contents

What would you attempt to do if you knew you could not fail? ~Unknown

On Your Own 101

Things You Forgot of Were Never Taught

Introduction

These tips, tricks and suggestions originally came together when I realized as a parent with as many things which I had taught my children, there was still necessary preparation for them to move out of the house. So many things that had been done for them and not taught to them. Upon this realization it was clear that in many ways my children were not nearly as prepared for the basics in the real world as they need to be. They know how to call us, they know how to ask for a ride, they know how to use every technological instrument known to man but they don't know how to use a toilet plunger or jumper cables. I am pretty sure Xbox live will not be able to send aid in the event of an emergency or unexpected uh-oh.

As I began talking about the content during the writing process, so many people began confessing that they didn't know how to do many of the simple tasks I was including. Thus, this book is not just for young adults moving out on their own for the first time but for anyone and everyone. There is at least one topic in this book that will bail you out of a jam.

Whether you are a new "renter" because of today's economic changes or are seeking a new roommate for the first time, there are things you need to know to cover yourself from beginning to end, financially and emotionally. You will find some of those answers along with so many others in this book

One reviewer suggested that everyone should have two copies, one in the house and one in the car with the "automobile" section being so important.

I really just want to be sure that my kids were prepared, but I also want to be help anyone who is facing a new challenge in life. This book is meant to bring back to focus the fundamental things we will encounter in life and how to get them done. It is a step by step, easy to follow, no nonsense helpful resource guide.

Knowledge is a gift that can't be taken away. Experience is a process. This book brings together my knowledge and experience to help you have an easier road when confronted with life's little adventures and perhaps stumbling blocks. It's a "how to" so you can are able to say, "I can do that, no problem" and you can help someone else because "It's no big deal"

Here's to life's adventures with a manual to help you along the way!

Welcome to the Neighborhood

You are on the search for a place to live or you think you have found the location you'd like to live in…now how do you make it a reality?

- Roommates

- Rental applications

- Utilities

- What's in your neighborhood

- How do you get around

Be prepared, efficient and successful from beginning to end in your search for the perfect place for you.

Looking for an Apartment

Roommates are the people you share housing with whether in the same room or in the same dwelling. Consider how much time each day you have spent living under the same roof with your family, this is the same amount of time you will likely be sharing living space with a roommate or roommates.

With that in mind, it is important that you find people you are compatible with in order to experience a pleasant living arrangement.

Places to search for a roommate and or advertise for one:

- School campus

- Your local religious organization

- Craigslist.com

- Roommate Finders

- Newspaper

- Ask friends

- Your job

- Roommate placement agencies

If you are meeting a stranger as a potential candidate, who has responded to an advertisement you placed, be extremely cautious. Always meet in a public place like a coffee shop. Bring a trusted friend; this way you are not alone and they can later share their opinion about this person as a potential roommate.

When you have decided that this person may be a viable roommate you will need to show them the living space. At the time you are showing your home to this potential roommate have a minimum of two friends present if you are a female, and at least one friend present if you are a male. People do prey upon people advertising for roommates and rentals. When dealing with strangers, it is always better to be safe than sorry.

If you feel that this person is 'the one' it is critical that you conduct a thorough background check and reference check before you make any commitments. (See the section on check roommate references to make sure you cover all the bases.)

Even with a complete check you can still run into issues, nothing is fool proof or fail safe. Knowing someone who knows your potential roommate personally and is willing to be honest with you about their compatibility to you is generally your best bet.

Filling out a Rental Application

Arriving prepared will increase your chances of securing the new place you have chosen for home. Filling out a rental application is much like a job application in that you will be asked for personal information, likely drivers license number, social security number and references. Your references should include your employer, current and past; your previous rental history and contact information as well as personal references. Bring along with you all of this information so you can complete the application on site. It will also help you to make a good impression as a responsible potential tenant. If you will be sharing the home/apartment, all of the tenants may be asked to complete an application. Be sure you share this information with your roommates so you are all in alignment with your preparedness.

You will also want to have a checkbook with you to leave a check for the credit report which will be run by the property management company or owner. This fee to check your credit report usually runs $20-50 (see credit report section of this book for making sure you are going to show up with good results).

If you fill out an application and leave a check, ask when you can expect to hear back from the results. If you have not heard back in the time promised, follow up with a call.

Present yourself in a professional manner for the first impression. A clean tidy appearance is important. Remember these individuals are about to hand over keys to a home or apartment worth a lot of money and they want to feel comfortable knowing they are making a good decision by putting their trust in you.

Pre-move in Inspection

Once you are approved and are preparing to move in to your new place, be sure to do a walk-through with the management. For your best protection make notes of any pre-existing damages, marks on the walls, etc. It is recommended that you take pictures to keep on file in case there is any question of how the property looked upon arrival and departure. These pictures have stood up in court when a tenant was not guilty of damage that was being charged against their departure. It's for your protection.

Finding a Roommate

The best place to begin your search for a roommate is by asking your friends, local relatives, co-workers and schoolmates for recommendations. If these resources fail to turn up the right person, you can then begin the search for a stranger online at Craigslist.com, Roommates.com or any other local forum that advertises for house sharing. There are also agencies that do roommate placements. This is a good way to go if you don't want to do the reference check, credit reports, etc. Agencies usually match people with similar desires…of course, this will cost you, but in the long run it could also save you a lot of hassle and money.

Should you choose someone online or who has not been screened professionally? Do yourself a huge favor and follow the guidelines under the *Checking References for Roomates* section of this book. It is much easier to pass on a potential housemate than it is to get rid of a horrible roommate (that hassle could lead you in some cases to court and a huge financial burden).

Checking References for Roommates

It's always easiest if your roommate is referred to you by someone you know and trust, but even then you should get a rental application from your local office supply store or online and have the potential candidate complete it. Once you have the information, verify everything listed including personal references, job references, previous living situations, banking information, etc. In short, check every bit of information they provide.

When you are checking references, ask the following types of questions:

- Would you rent to them again?

- Would you hire them again?

- Did you have any problems that I should be concerned about?

- Did they pay on time each month?

- Were they responsible?

- Did they give you proper notice when they moved out?

- Did they leave the premises in the same condition in which it was rented?

- Did they have any unusual habits, any pets, do they smoke?"

Be aware that potential renters and or references may tell you what they think you want to hear. Probe past the surface and follow your instincts. If you are remiss in asking key questions before someone moves in and problems arise, it is neither easy, nor fun to have to terminate a living situation.

Be clear on what works for each of you before you make a commitment. Find out if you have similar sleeping and waking hours, interests, music tastes, and respect for others. Are you compatible with this person you are considering living with? It's about so much more than just finding someone to pay part of the rent.

Utilities

If you are renting an apartment and you are the first roommate to get things started, you will need to find out from your landlord which utilities are NOT included in your monthly rent. Once you know what you are responsible for, you can begin the process of calling the various companies and setting up accounts to have service begin on or just before your move in date.

Services likely to be covered in an apartment complex:

- Water

- Sewer

- Garbage

Services you will likely need to set up and pay on your own:

- Cable

- Electricity/Gas

- Telephone

Ask your landlord for the numbers to the local services, they should be able to provide this contact information. Check to see if you are able to arrange a payment plan in addition to your monthly statement for deposits on utilities to make it more affordable at move in.

Opening a Utility Account

First you need to know from your landlord which utilities you are responsible for paying each month, from there you begin the process of contacting those companies. Utilities include: sewer, water, garbage, electricity, cable, telephone, propane, and internet services. Some of the services are paid for by the landlord when you are renting or leasing an apartment. Most of them are not when you are renting/leasing a house.

Once you have learned what you are responsible for, get the phone numbers to the local providers and start making your calls before you move in. There will likely be a setup fee, along with a deposit, if it is your first time to establish services. Many companies may run a credit check and this may help determine if they will require a deposit; many companies require a deposit regardless. Keep this in mind when you are budgeting for a move.

When you call to set up service at a new residence, you will either be requesting a new account, or if you have moved within the same service area, you will be requesting a transfer of service. The representative will be able to help you set up the account which best serves your needs. Be sure to ask if there is a discount if you bundle services, for instance through the phone or cable company. You should compare pricing even if you don't have a landline telephone in the home.

Note: One small, but potentially big thing to think about when deciding if you want a landline: how likely is the possibility that there would be an emergency at your home which would require emergency services to locate your home without being given the address? For instance, if you are the reason for the call there may not be anyone in your home who would know the address. This is the one thing that a cell phone cannot provide unless it has GPS activated.

Things You Should Know About Your Neighborhood

- Your physical address and nearest cross street to your house or apartment.

- Where is the closest fire station?

- What is the crime rate in your neighborhood?

- Where is the closest grocery store and pharmacy?

- Where is the nearest hospital?

- Are there school zones…think speed traps.

- What is the garbage pickup day and do you need to put the cans at the curb?

- What time is the mail usually delivered?

- Where is the nearest dry cleaner or laundry mat if you don't have a washer/dryer at your home?

- Which nearby coffee shops offer free Wi-Fi?

- What is the nearest pizzeria and other restaurants that deliver and their phone numbers?

Changing Your Mailing Address

Go to your local post office and pick up a change of address form; fill it out completely according to the instructions and hand it in at the post office window or drop it in a mailbox. You can also change your address online for a small fee at the United States Postal Service's website.

It will generally take at least a week for the mail to be forwarded, so if you are waiting for something time sensitive, make sure you either wait until it has arrived or give yourself plenty of time by changing the address well in advance of its expected arrival.

Getting a New Doctor

It's likely that your parents have always made your medical arrangements, and hopefully you are still under their health care coverage. If not, you need to find out how you can get coverage...through your job, school, etc? If medical coverage is not an option, find out which offices operate on a sliding scale (varied charges based upon one's income and ability to pay).

Once you know how your medical bills will likely be covered, check to see if there are specific physicians who are covered under your insurance plan and where they have offices in close proximity to your home.

You will no longer be seeing your life long pediatrician, you are now an adult and outside of their scope of practice. Decide if you prefer a male or female caregiver, if you have that flexibility and then call to schedule a "get to know you" consultation before you are sick. Establish a relationship with the doctor so you feel comfortable calling in a time of need.

Be sure you know the hours of the clinic or office and how you can reach the doctor after hours in case of emergency. Locate the closest after hours urgent care center and hospital. Remember if there is a life threatening situation, always dial 911 first. They will take it from there.

Extra Keys

Always have an extra set of keys to your car, your home and mailbox if you use a post office box. Keys can usually be made at your local hardware store inexpensively. Keep the keys in a safe place and let someone you trust know where they can be found in case yours are lost, stolen, locked in your car, or in the case of an emergency.

Getting a New Drivers License

Go online and research your state's licensing procedure for changing your address. If you are in the same state, you may be able to make a simple address change online. If you are in a new state, you may be required to test in that state, usually written, but possibly a driving test as well. The information will be listed on the Department of Licensing website for that state. Find the nearest office to your new location, and if necessary, call or go in to make an appointment.

You will need your old identification or current driver's license, proof of address (a utility bill or rental agreement will usually suffice) and proof of auto insurance. Again, all of the required documents and steps to follow should be found on the state's licensing website.

Many states have deadlines for changing your address or switching your license to the state in which you are living. Failure to comply will result in a sizable fine if you are caught. Don't delay; just get it done…who knows you could end up with a better picture!

Getting a Passport

You now need a passport to travel to Canada and Mexico. The government passport agency recommends that you allow yourself six to eight weeks lead time before your scheduled travel to get your first passport or renew your current passport. There is an expedited service available at an additional cost. This usually requires you to go to a passport office (you can locate the nearest office with an online search).

You may need to provide documentation of your intended travel to utilize the expedited service. When you are visiting the passport office website, be sure to make note of the items you will need to have with you, which will include passport pictures taken elsewhere (these are special pictures with specific dimensions you will give to the passport office for them to process your request). You will also need proof of who you are; the website has a list of the acceptable forms, be sure you are prepared or you will waste a lot of time and leave disappointed instead of anticipating the arrival of your freedom to travel outside the country.

Air Travel

When you are traveling by air, there are basic guidelines that you must follow or you will not be able to travel. The airlines recommend arriving two hours prior to the scheduled departure for check in. Make sure you have with you, official photo identification (i.e.: driver's license or passport unless you are under 18, photo identification is not required 0-18 years old) and either your printed e-ticket, if you have checked in online before arriving at the airport, or your confirmation number if you are checking in at the airport.

It's always good to carry some cash when you are traveling for any unforeseen expenses, such as gratuities for porters or snacks; but it is essential to make sure you have a means of payment if you are checking in luggage. Most airlines now charge anywhere from $20-50 even for your first checked bag. This means pack carefully, carry on what you are able (making sure you follow the security guidelines when packing) so you are not held up or have your items taken away when you go through security.

You can check for guidelines by going to TSA.gov (Transportation Security Administration) and on most airline websites. There are many items which you cannot carry on, but you may check through security. The complete list is found at www.TSA.gov. With carry-on items, liquids and aerosols (this also includes toothpaste and fragrances) are permitted as carry-on items with the following restrictions:

No more than 3.4 oz (100ml) bottle or less by volume; all liquids must be contained and placed on the security belt in a quart-sized, clear plastic, zip-top bag and only one plastic bag is permitted per passenger. It must be placed outside of your luggage on the security belt.

Additionally, computers must be removed from their cases and set in a bin separately for inspection before passing through security. Be courteous to fellow travelers by having your belongings organized for an expeditious trip through security. Shoes, jackets, most belts and some jewelry will need to be removed; keep this in mind when you are dressing for your journey. Keep it simple and plan for easy on and off.

Using Public Transportation

Taxis, trains, buses, ferries, and subways are excellent cost effective transportation methods. Public transportation runs on schedules, unlike a taxi they are not always readily available when you need them, so you need to locate a schedule either online or at a bus stop, subway, and train or ferry station.

31

Public transportation requires more planning, as you are not in control of the timing. Websites for each method generally provide time of travel between destinations along with stop/pick up times at each pick up location. They also inform you of any closures, delays, or last minute schedule reconfigurations. Figure out when you need to arrive at your destination and then work backwards to determine when you need to begin your journey.

Using public transportation is not as scary as it may seem, do it once and you will see that it can actually be a relaxing and affordable way to travel. You do need to be aware of your surroundings and use common sense. When you are traveling on or waiting for public transportation, be sure to pay attention to what and who is around you. These areas of clustered people can be an easy place for pick pockets and other small crimes. Don't allow yourself to become a victim because you are not paying attention.

Hailing a Cab

It seems like hailing a cab would be simple, but there is nothing more frustrating than standing on a corner or street and being ignored by a passing taxi cab. If the cab has passengers (a fare) already, you will absolutely be ignored. So patience is important, again, plan ahead if you are on a timeline, call ahead and ask for a pick up at your desired location. If you are taking a chance to be spotted and picked up, stand on the edge of the street or corner, keep your eyes open and when you see a taxi coming your way, wave your hand and do your best to make eye contact with the driver so they don't think you are just waving to a friend. Be sure you are looking both directions for an oncoming cab; they will often make a U-turn to pick you up. They need to eat and you are their bread and butter, even if in some cities it doesn't seem that way. Always remember that taxi drivers will expect (and it is common courtesy to give) a gratuity of 15% on top of the fare. Research the laws in your state. In some states, such as Utah, it is illegal to hail a cab from the street; you have to call the cab company in advance for pickup.

Caring for Your Home - Cleanliness Counts!

Your mother doesn't live here and she isn't stocking the kitchen or cleaning up behind you. All of the things which may have been done for you in the past are now your own responsibility. You shouldn't live in a pig pen, dine on bread and water alone, and you may even want to entertain…here's how!

Bed Linens

Changing the linens on your bed should NOT be done just when you are expecting company, but at least twice a month, only if you shower regularly and go to bed CLEAN! If that's not the case, you need to change sheets weekly.

To ensure that you are able to do this, you should have more than one set of sheets. A "set" of sheets consists of a fitted sheet, top or flat sheet and a pillow case or two depending on the sheet size and numbers of pillows on the bed. All sizes (except twin size) come with two pillow cases. You should also have two mattress pads. A mattress pad is a cover that goes over the mattress under the sheet to protect the bed and smooth out the surface making it more comfortable to sleep on.

Properly Making a Bed

Strip the bed of all covers and the pillows of all their cases. First, put a fresh mattress pad on the mattress; pay attention so you are putting the correct side on the bed. Next put on the fitted sheet. This is the sheet which has elastic around its edges and will never fold flat. Stretch and pull tight on each corner; pull the corners to cover the bottom edge of mattress so the sheet stays in place. Next, put the top sheet on the bed, right side DOWN with the wider hem at the top or head of the bed. Center the sheet so there are equal amounts of sheet hanging from each side. Now tuck the excess at the foot of the bed under the foot of the mattress. If you like the sheets tight on you, also tuck in the sides. Add a blanket, a comforter or bedspread. Place pillow cases on the pillows and place them on top of a comforter or tucked in under the bed spread. If you want a tidier feeling when you come home each day, at least pull the sheet and blankets up each day and put the pillows in place. It's sort of making the bed...

A Really Clean Bathroom

If you don't really care about how clean your bathroom is, think about this, if you have a guest over and he or she goes into your bathroom (and they will), it is a direct reflection of your cleanliness. In other words, if your bathroom is dirty, that "maybe" someone special will think perhaps your lack of cleanliness is not confined to your bathroom or bedroom or kitchen, but also your personal hygiene as well. Clean bathroom, clean kitchen, clean sheets…clean mind ;).

The Cleaning Process

Choose a bathroom cleaning solution that pleases your nose. There are some that are really overwhelming and others that smell really clean. (Do NOT mix solutions together; this can cause deadly, toxic fumes). Pick one for each surface or one for every surface and stick with it. Some are all-in-ones, in other words, they are fine for cleaning the shower and they spray safely on your kitchen counter. Make sure you do not wear clothing that could be damaged if you get cleaning solution on them. It's a good idea to choose a set of clothes that you only wear when you are cleaning; this is your cleaning outfit. Wear gloves with it if you prefer. Be sure to put away your toothbrush away so it doesn't become contaminated with cleaner. Clear everything off of the counter, the back of the toilet and the floor of the shower or the sides of the tub. Sweep the floor before any surfaces get wet.

Spray or shake the cleaner all over the shower/tub and sink. Let it sit while you spray down the toilet seat, under the seat, behind the seat and on top of the tank. Squirt cleanser on the inside of the toilet bowl, then use a toilet brush with a long handle to scrub and clean the bowl…all the way down the drain, as far as your brush fits. Now, with a paper towel so as not to spread germs with a rag, wipe every sprayed surface clean. Next, spray the mirror with glass cleaner and wipe clean. Once all of the surfaces are clean and germ free you might need to rinse residual film away with water. Finally use a floor cleaner (usually mixed with water) and with a mop or on your hands and knees with a cloth, wash the floor. Don't forget to clean the base of the toilet when you are washing the floor...this area can often be a catch for all of the "drips" and should not be missed when cleaning. Once the floor is clean, be sure there is a roll of toilet paper on the paper holder with a spare under the sink or within sight, layout fresh towels, and put a clean hand towel on the towel rack or loop. A clean bathroom will impress all and makes it that much more pleasant for your own personal use.

Because your bathroom is definitely a room which will be utilized by guests, you want to present it not only clean, but also appealing and well stocked for your guests' needs. Make it attractive with nice towels, candles, air freshener, feminine care products for female guests and even condoms (these items can be stored out of sight).

Cleaning a Floor

Before attempting to clean any floor, determine the surface type; is it wood, tile, vinyl, etc. Is it a hard surface that you can sweep with a broom or is it carpet that you must vacuum?

Sweeping is only the first step to cleaning a hard surface floor. If your floor is hardwood, be sure to use only a cleaner specifically designed for hardwood cleaning like Murphy's Hardwood Cleaner. For other surfaces like linoleum, tile, Pergo (manmade wood surface that is tile-like), or concrete look for a cleanser in the cleaning aisle of the grocery store designed for those surfaces.

Know what surface you are cleaning and buy the correct product. Read the directions to see if you must dilute the product with water in a bucket or if it is to be applied directly to the floor. There are also commercial products like Swiffer, a mop like tool that has the cleanser attached for one step cleaning without the hassle of a mop and without the need to rinse.

Carpet Care

Carpets need to be shampooed periodically, either professionally or with a rental machine from carpet or grocery stores. Do it yourself carpet cleaning (not so much fun and sometimes not very effective) can be messy. Keep your carpet cleaner by asking guests to remove shoes and being careful with drinks and food on carpeted areas. Do not let your friends make more work for you!

Changing a Vacuum Cleaner Bag

Changing a vacuum bag is necessary when the vacuum is actually used. Typically, a vacuum cleaner has an indicator on the top of the canister somewhere that is red or green. If you notice that it is red, this means it is full and you need to replace the bag in order for the vacuum to have suction to pick up the dirt. You can also open the canister and feel if the bag is full. If it is, replace it with a new bag.

Bags are available for purchase at most major variety stores, Target, Wal-Mart and Sears and some larger grocery store chains. All you need to know is the make and model of your vacuum cleaner or better yet, the bag size and model listed on the full bag in your machine.

The bag usually slips in and out of grooves designed to hold the bag in place. If you use a machine with a bag that is full you run the risk of burning up the motor and ruining the machine. Even if you don't burn up the motor, if the bag is too full, the job will not get done properly and the bag may possibly burst leaving you a bigger mess!

If you have a bag-less vacuum cleaner, pay attention to the full indicator and empty as it is needed otherwise the unit will stop picking up dirt and may actually begin spitting dirt out. If you notice that there is suction, but the brush is not spinning and not grabbing dirt, check to see if there is a missing or broken belt, which can be purchased and replaced where the machines or bags are sold. Some lesser expensive machines do not have a belt, check yours out or refer to the owner's manual for belt part number and additional replacement instructions.

Washing Clothes

To avoid ruining your clothes, these are some simple steps to follow.

Sort your clothing by colors…whites with whites, dark with darks (black, navy, dark brown etc.), light colored clothing separate from brights. Be sure you pull out any clothing which is hand wash only…these items will be handled differently.

Almost all clothing has a label with recommended washing instructions; take a look if there is an item of concern otherwise a good rule of thumb for water temperature is as follows:

- Linens, towels - Hot water wash

- Most clothing (unless you are concerned about shrinkage) - Warm water wash.

- If shrinkage (high cotton content, linen silk, wool content) is a concern, you should use cold water wash.

- Many "hand wash only" items can often be washed on the delicate cycle with cold water.

- Items which should not go into the washing machine include anything leather or fur.

- Plastic, vinyl, and 'pleather' items can usually go in the washing machine but never in the dryer (these items can melt).

Be cautious with washing wool, cashmere and rayon items as they are likely to shrink; (if in doubt, hand wash). If you do choose to wash any of these materials, always only use cold water and lay out to dry; do not put them in a dryer.

Place separated load into the washing machine and disperse it evenly. If using a top loading machine, be sure you have not overloaded the drum. Top loaders are at capacity when the tub is ½

41

-3/4 filled; front loaders can be crammed full; however keep in mind the wet weight of towels or jeans could impact the cycle. Don't go crazy and put in 10 pairs of jeans or 20 towels just because they fit in the dryer. Your clothes will not get clean if you over stuff a washing machine. Keep this in mind especially with smaller apartment sized machines.

Pour the indicated amount of laundry detergent in the detergent drawer or in the washing machine as per instructions on the bottle or box. Again, do not use any soaps which are not made for washing clothes and do not use more than recommended to avoid bubbles rolling out on to the floor. Do not pour bleach directly on any clothing. If you use chlorine bleach, unless it says color safe, it will likely bleach all color out of anything it comes in contact with, including anything you are wearing.

Sour Clothes

You have left a load in the washing machine too long and there is now a sour smell. If you transfer them to the dryer at this point, you will seal in the sour smell until the laundry is washed again. To eliminate the odor simply wash them again in detergent and also add a ½ cup of baking soda or borax which helps to extinguish smells. This is also good if your clothes smell from other odors such as fish, grease, smoke, etc.

Using the Dryer

On most machines, there are automatic cycles to choose from. Select the cycle which is most appropriate for the load you are putting in the dryer. Be sure you always clean the lint filter. It is usually found inside the dryer door or on top of the dryer. It is a screen which traps lint between loads and will impact the efficiency of your dryer's operation if it is not cleared between each load.

It's a personal choice to use dryer sheets. These are good if you experience a lot of static electricity and it also helps to reduce wrinkles as clothing is drying. They are available with or without fragrances for people with sensitivities or allergies.

Dry Cleaning

Coats and other clothing labels stating "dry clean only", without the option of hand washing including suits, men's dress slacks, silk blouses, most dresses, leather, suede, evening gowns, beaded and sequined or heavily embellished garments all require special cleaning. Cashmere and wool sweaters are also best cleaned professionally.

There is an at home alternative for lighter weight items if you have access to a clothes dryer. Dryel sheets, sold at supermarkets and variety stores, is a 'home' system which allows you to throw your garments in the dryer bag supplied along with the special "dry cleaning" sheet.

Follow instructions on the box. This is a great way to have your garments fresh without the cost of dry cleaning after each wearing. This product works great if your clothes are not "dirty" or heavily soiled or musty with body odor and is perfect in- between professional cleanings. Be sure your dryer is set on the proper setting indicated on the product directions to avoid damage to your clothes.

Removing Stains from Clothing

Figure out what kind of stain is in the article of clothing. Is it a grease stain, juice, wine, sandwich condiments, coffee, ink, blood or chewing gum? We've all fallen victim to most of these and they are each removed differently. Make sure you know what that stain is so you know how to best treat it.

For grease stains, scrape off the excess solids with a butter knife. Place the stain face down on a plain white paper towel. Squeeze a small amount of dishwashing liquid on the underside of the stain to break up the grease; Dawn liquid detergent works the best (hey, it works on dishes), and wait about a minute. Pre-treat the stain with detergent, and wash it on the warmest water setting that particular fabric can endure.

For juices, wines, coffee, tomato-based sauces and soft drinks, blot the stain with cold water. Then, sprinkle the stain with salt to absorb any liquid. After a moment or two, wipe clean with club soda and pre-treat for a wash cycle.

To get rid of chewing gum, rub the glob of goo with ice to harden it. Then scrape it off with a dull knife (butter knife works great) and wash.

For ink, hold the portion of garment tight over the top of a glass or wide mouth jar. Pour rubbing alcohol slowly over the stain, with your piece of clothing acting as a sieve. Rinse and wash as usual.

Check the stain for complete removal before placing any clothing article in the dryer. The heat from the dryer will "set" the stain and it will become permanent. If stain remains prior to laundering, repeat the stain removal process once more.

For most other stains, rinse, treat with stain remover and launder as usual. One exception is nail polish, which you should first rub with acetone nail polish remover. Then send it through the laundry cycle.

Ironing

One of the easiest ways to reduce the need to iron your clothes is to be sure you are drying them in the clothes dryer on the appropriate temperature (too hot can create more wrinkles). Even more important is to remove them from the dryer and shake them out, fold them or hang them on a hanger as soon as the dryer has stopped, while the clothes are still warm. Taking them from the dryer and throwing them in a basket for a folding "party" later only results in a basket of wrinkles. Save yourself the trouble.

For things that do need to be ironed because of the fabric (or because they were left in the basket), it is best to use an ironing board; although, in a pinch, you can use a towel on the floor or bed as an ironing surface. Look at the fabric content on the label of the item to be ironed and turn the iron to the indicated setting.

If your iron has a water tank, fill the tank to the maximum water fill level. This will allow you to push the steam button or spray button for extra stubborn wrinkles and for quicker wrinkle release. Do not try to use a hotter iron than directed on delicate fabrics, leather, plastic, etc to get the job done quicker. You will ruin the garment.

If you burn something with the bottom of the iron you must clean the iron before using it on another item. If you don't, you will likely deposit permanent marks on the garment creating indelible black or brown stains.

Cleaning an Iron

Nonstick Surface: (the iron's surface looks like non-stick pans in the kitchen)

- Clean with a scotch, soft abrasive scrubber

- Paper bag method: pour salt on a paper bag and run hot iron over the salt.

- Wax paper method: same as paper bag method; except using wax paper to coat the bottom of the iron for a smoother glide as you are cleaning.

Metal Surface:

- Brillo pad, Steel wool pad

- Wax paper: see above

- Paper bag:see above

Commercial iron cleansers are essentially a non-oily, non-abrasive liquid or gel soap similar to Dawn dishwashing liquid.

When you are finished using your iron, TURN THE IRON OFF and unplug it. Never leave an iron in a place where it is touching anything which could catch fire if the iron were to automatically turn on or be left on. (Many irons turn on if they are plugged in and are triggered by movement.)

Mending a Tear and Sewing on a Button

Wearing clothes that are tattered or torn and are not the pre-torn fashion, is not cool. Buy a travel size sewing kit from a drug/variety store or linen store and keep it on hand. They usually have a small amount of enough colors of thread to get you through a bind and they include a couple of needles, safety pins, straight pins to hold fabric together and sometimes even a measuring tape meant to measure fabric not wood. Don't forget to also buy a pair of scissors.

When you begin mending clothes or sewing on a button, pull about 12 inches of thread off of the spool, thread the needle in the tiny hole (eye), pull the thread through the eye so the ends meet, and tie a small knot.

Now you are ready to tackle the hole. Insert the needle from the back side of the fabric so you know it is not on the outside of the repair. It's as easy as up on one side, down on the other moving along the tear until it is repaired. Try and sew in as straight a line as possible. End on a downward movement so you can pull tight and knot off out of sight to complete the job. Sewing on a button goes the same way only you are attaching something on the upward movement.

All of the Details

Moving is up there on the stress scale but you can take it down a notch or two by preparing and knowing what you need to about your new environment. Things are not always as they seem so you have to take it upon yourself to find out before you find yourself in a bind. Do your homework, save yourself headaches and a growling stomach.

Stocking Your New Home

Here is a shopping list of essentials you will need to properly suit your new place:

- Towels for the bathroom, at least four bath sized towels

- Hand towels, at least four

- Wash cloths, at least four

- Linens for your bed, at least two sets of sheets

- A Blanket and a comforter or bedspread

- Pillows, at least two

- A table for eating with chairs (and maybe studying)

- Seating in the living room: chairs, couch, bean bags, something besides the floor

- A bed

- Nightstand

- Lamps

- Desk or place to study…could be the multi-purpose kitchen table

- A place to store your clothes

- Wastebaskets for kitchen, bathroom and bedroom

- Window coverings if there are no blinds

- A broom and a mop

- Vacuum cleaner

- Cleaning supplies such as carpet cleaner, Windex, all-purpose cleaner

Making the Grocery List for the Supermarket

- Bread, Bagels and Tortillas

- Bread Crumbs

- Butter or Margarine

- Broth-chicken, beef and vegetable

- Canned Tuna

- Cereal hot & cold

- Cheese

- Coffee & Tea

- Crushed Tomatoes

- Eggs

- Frozen quick foods

- Lemon & Lime juice (fresh or bottled)

- Milk & Juice

- Pancake Mix (Just add water)

- Pastas (spaghetti, penne, macaroni…etc.)

- Pasta Sauce (marinara or tomato basil)

- Peanut Butter & Jelly

- Rice-Uncle Bens or Minute Rice is quickest to prepare

- Soups-canned or in the cardboard containers

- Tomato Paste

- Baking Soda

- Baking powder

- Cooking Oil (canola, vegetable, olive)
- Cornstarch
- Flour
- Ketchup
- Mayonnaise
- Mustard
- Soy Sauce
- Sugar (cane and brown)
- Vinegar (balsamic, apple cider and white distilled)
- Salt and Pepper
- Cinnamon
- Paprika
- Basil
- Cayenne Pepper
- Garlic Powder
- Onion Powder
- Oregano
- Italian blend of seasonings
- Garlic either chopped or powdered
- Oregano
- Chili powder
- Thyme
- Cinnamon

- Vanilla
- Flour
- Salad dressing
- Eggs
- Storage and freezer bags in both quart and gallon size
- Wax paper
- Tin foil
- **Plastic wrap**

Stocking the Kitchen

While it is nice to have brand new items, if you are on a budget, check out second hand stores, garage sales and don't forget the dollar store! Spend your money decorating instead.

Storage and Cleanup

- Plastic storage containers, not necessarily microwaveable, various sizes

- Canisters with tight fitting lids for cereal, coffee, flour, sugar, dried pasta

- Kitchen towels

- Scouring pads suitable for nonstick pots and pans

- Oven cleaner, Liquid dish washing soap and if you are lucky, dishwasher detergent

- All-purpose spray cleanser for stove tops, counter and sink

- Broom

- Dust pan

- Mop

- Bucket

Basics Cooking Tools

- Microwave
- Toaster
- Coffee maker
- Hand mixer
- Can opener
- Skillets-one 10-12" and one smaller 6-8"
- Covered sauté pan
- Small sauce pot
- 2 quart pot
- 4-5 quart pot
- Casserole/Baking dishes
- 1 muffin pan
- 2 Cookie sheets
- Pizza pan or stone1 broiling pan
- Durable microwavable containers with lids for heating and for storage…you can get these is three sizes usually in sets.
- At least 2 serving spoons, both slotted and non-slotted
- Spatulas
- Scrapers
- Pasta servers (a nice extra to have) and tongs
- A good knife set in its own block

- Kitchen scissors if they do not come with the knife set Measuring cups both liquid (usually plastic or glass) and dry (usually plastic or metal

- Measuring spoons

- Ice cream scoop

- Salad tongs

- Cork screw

- Mixing bowls-buy a set so that they fit inside each other for stackable storage.

- Two oven mitts or pot holders.

Get Cooking!

It is cheaper to eat 'in' than to eat out all the time. The fastest way to gain weight is to frequent the dollar menu at your favorite fast food spot. Mom was right, "Homemade is best!" Nothing tastes better than a good burger on the grill or a fresh salad topped with your favorites. So roll up your sleeves and wash your hands and let's get cooking!

Grilling a Hamburger

The best burgers are made from fresh ground beef or sirloin rather than a frozen pre-pressed, already formed burger. Figure on purchasing about ½ pound of meat per burger as you are buying, to factor in shrinkage as you grill. Multiply the number of guests times .5 to know how many pounds of ground meat you will need. So, 2 people times .50 equals 1 pound. When you are buying ground beef for burgers, for better flavor choose the beef with a higher fat content percentage; 8% fat vs. 4% makes a juicer burger.

Turn your grill on to medium/high and preheat; be sure it is cleaned after each use so it is ready to use when you are ready to eat. Make sure you have propane in the tank when using a gas grill and that all connections are tight to avoid leakage. Most gas grills have electric starter buttons and that is all it takes to get a flame, once you have turned the burners on and released the propane to the burners below the grill.

While the grill preheats, wash your hands in hot soapy water and make your burger patties. Mix the raw meat in a bowl with some of your favorite seasonings: a little salt, pepper, small amount of barbeque sauce, Worchester sauce. Mix together well with a spoon or with clean bare hands (this works best). Next, shape meat into ½ inch thick patties about 4 inches in diameter. Place formed patties on a plate to transport to grill. Once you have placed the burgers on the grill, turn heat to medium and watch the burgers sizzle. For safe eating, burgers should be cooked medium-well although some prefer them rarer (or less cooked) than this. Medium-well is achieved by grilling a burger on a medium hot grill for about 3-4 minutes on each side.

To avoid food borne illness the internal temperature recommended by the FDA for beef is 165°, this can be checked with a food thermometer. You can also use a knife to cut in the middle of a burger to check the color. Medium is light pink in the middle, medium well is barely pink and no pink is well done.

If you want to add cheese, place sliced cheese on top of the burger as it is almost done for it to melt. If you like your buns warm, place them on the top shelf of the grill as you add the cheese. They toast quickly so it only takes a few moments. Remove your buns and place your grilled patties on each bun.

Never place buns or cooked burgers on the plate that you used for the raw meat unless it has been washed with soap and hot water. If you do, it is a quick way to possibly experience food poisoning and/or other food borne illnesses like E. coli.

Cooking Pasta

1. Fill a large, deep pot with water according to the number of servings you desire.

2. Add a few shakes of salt (about 1/8th of a teaspoon).

3. Bring water to a rolling, bubbling boil.

4. Add pasta to water, refer to box for amount of pasta to water.

5. Allow to boil uncovered.

6. Stir to break apart pasta that clumps and keep it from sticking together.

7. It will return to a boil, stir frequently.

8. Boil for 8 – 10 minutes total, do not overcook or it will be mushy. Test a piece of pasta by pulling it and tasting. Pasta should be firm but not crunchy or mushy.

9. All varieties of pasta, spaghetti, ziti, bowtie and egg noodles differ in cooking times, check the package for guidelines.

10. Drain pasta in a colander (a bowl with holes in the bottom), rinse first under cold water, and rinse a second time with hot water if you are serving under sauce. For pasta salads, rinse only once in cold water and drain thoroughly.

Transfer cooked and drained pasta to a mixing bowl if you are making a pasta salad and add your favorite ingredients.

Transfer to a baking dish if you are making a casserole.

Transfer to a bowl if you plan to serve it with a separate sauce like marinara, Alfredo or other pasta sauce. Drizzle and mix with a very small amount of olive oil to keep it from sticking together before adding sauce especially if you are serving the pasta and sauce separately.

Enjoy the pasta with olive oil and parmesan cheese tossed with a few fresh steamed vegetables for a quick, healthy meal. (Steam veggies quickly by tossing them in the bottom of the colander just prior to dumping in pasta and boiling water, perfect for broccoli or cauliflower.)

Meatballs can also be made or purchased in the frozen section pre-made ready for heating.

Make it a real meal by adding a quick green salad (lettuce of your choice, chopped tomatoes and any other vegetables you like) and a loaf of French bread warmed in the oven spread with butter and sprinkled with garlic powder or pre- made, ready to heat garlic bread found in the frozen section or bakery of your supermarket.

Cooking an Egg

- Fried Egg: Heat a skillet or frying pan on a medium heat setting, melting a bit of margarine or butter in the bottom of the pan; when it is melted fully, spread it around the pan. Crack your egg gently on the side of the pan and open it into the pan on the butter. Eggs are fried to varying degrees and people are very particular about how they like their eggs done.

- Sunny side up: Fried without flipping and a very runny yolk and runny white outer edges.

- Over easy: Fried, flipping but with a very running yolk.

- Over medium: White part is hard and yolk is thick but not hard.

- Over hard: Entire egg is fried until it is solid.

- Scrambled: Heat the pan as if to fry but instead of gently cracking and sliding the egg into the pan, you will crack the eggs into a bowl, add a ½ or teaspoon of water and whip with a fork. Pour the mixed up egg into the skillet and season with salt, pepper or whatever else suits you. If you want to add shredded cheese you should do this as the eggs are almost done. Eggs will go from wet and watery to dry as they cook. Using a spatula, keep the eggs moving in the pan…otherwise you will end up with an omelet.

- Hard Boiled: Using a sauce pan or larger, deep pot (depending on the number of eggs you want to boil), fill the pan half way with water, and bring to a boil on high heat. Gently drop the eggs into the water…or use a big, plastic kitchen spoon and place them on the bottom of the pan. Let them boil until you see at least one of the eggs crack. Remove them from the heat, pour out the hot water, and let them cool (this can be done by running the eggs under cool water in a strainer). When you can touch them without burning your hands, carefully peel the shells to keep the egg intact. You can also store these cooked eggs in the fridge for 2-3 days for snacks or lunch.

- Soft boiled eggs: Are cooked the same way only less time. It is like a poached egg (see below) in a shell. They will have a hard white, outer egg and soft yolk inside.

- Poached eggs: Are cooked in water but not boiled. Poaching an egg is a way of getting similar results to a fried egg without the calories or cholesterol of frying. In a skillet add about ½ inch of water, bring to medium heat, crack the egg in the water and let it cook. You will see the white harden and then you will cook it until it is the desired yolk hardness. You can flip it over or brush water over the top to get a white topping.

Making a Salad

From the grocery store or fresh market, purchase the ingredients you want for your salad. There are many varieties of lettuce and salad greens from flavorless iceberg to rich earthy mixed variety field greens. Some of the most common varieties include romaine which is used to make a Caesar Salad but can be used for any salad, red and green leaf and butter lettuce to name a few. Along with choosing a lettuce, buy any other vegetables and fruits or nuts you enjoy. Consider buying cheese or lunch meats to add as well.

When preparing the lettuce, you must first wash it. If you purchase it in a bag that says it is thoroughly washed, consider washing it again anyway. Wash the lettuce with cool water and pat dry with a paper towel. To avoid bruising the clean drained lettuce if you really want to be a pro, tear your lettuce into bite size pieces like you would if you were tearing a piece of paper into bits and place lettuce in salad bowl. Chop the other ingredients into bite size pieces and add to the bowl of lettuce. Using your hands or salad tongs, toss all of the ingredients together.

If you have prepared your salad in advance of your meal or guests, wet and wring out a paper towel, place it over the bowl and put in the refrigerator. When you are ready to serve, you can decide if you want to add the dressing yourself or allow those indulging to add their own.

Kitchen Measurement Conversions

3 teaspoons (tsp/s) =1 Tablespoons (tbsp/s)

4 tbsps = ¼ cup

16 tbsps = 1 cup

4 ounces (oz) = ½ cup

8 oz. = 1 cup

16 oz. = 1 pound (lb.)

1 ounce = 2 Tablespoons

1(liquid)cup (c.)= ½ pint (pt.)

2 cups = 1 pt.

2 pints = 4 cups = 1 quart (qt.)

4 quarts = 1 gallon

Cup measurements to metric milliliters

1 cup = 237 ml

3/4 c. = 177 ml

2/3 c. = 158 ml

1/2 c. = 118 ml

1/3 c. = 79 ml

1/4 c. = 59 ml

1/8 c. = 30 ml

1/16 c. = 15 ml

Making a Pot of Coffee

Follow the instructions in the owner's manual for set up and filling of the reservoir. First, add the amount of water desired in the water reservoir. Place coffee filter in the filter basket. Add desired amount of coffee grounds. For stronger coffee, add more grounds. If you are using whole beans and grinding them yourself, set the grinder to automatic drip setting so your coffee is not too finely or too coarsely ground.

Food Spoilage and Expiration Dates

Eating food that is expired could have an unpleasant result: salmonella (also known as food poisoning), an illness one would not wish on their worst enemy. Most foods are required to have an expiration date; look on the side or bottom of the item and get rid of outdated items especially products containing egg, dairy or meat. A dead giveaway that food is past its prime is when they begin to look like a science project and either have mold growing on them or they have formed a solid when they are meant to be liquid...GROSS!

Keeping your refrigerator clean is as important as keeping your bathroom clean and changing your sheets regularly. If is out of date, it should be out of your house. This includes medications which have compromised efficacy and may not work as they are meant to if they are expired. Throw them out!

Using a Dishwasher

While having a dishwasher is a luxury to some, it is taken for granted by most. Loading a dishwasher correctly will maximize the effectiveness and eliminate wasted water.

Load the top rack with glasses, smaller bowls, small plates and over-sized kitchen utensils, large preparation knives and plastic items. (Be sure you check on anything which is not metal or glass to be sure it is marked dishwasher safe, otherwise you are taking a risk of ruining the item). On the bottom rack place larger plates, service bowls, pots and pans if they fit and are marked "dishwasher safe" and of course, forks, spoons and other utensils which are not too long in the smaller utensil basket. Once the dishwasher is loaded to capacity (but not so full that water cannot pass between items as this is how things get cleaned).

Next, you must add dishwasher detergent. This is different from *dishwashing* detergent! Dishwasher detergent comes in liquid and powder form, but it is NOT the same as the dish liquid you use to hand wash dishes. If you put dish washing liquid instead of dishwasher soap in a dishwasher, it will foam and bubble and you will find a huge mess of water and soap coming out of your dishwasher mid cycle. DO NOT make this mistake or you will be mopping up a ton of bubbles and water.

Cleaning a Stove and Oven

If you have a glass cook top, flat dark surface without any raised heating elements, you will need to purchase a cook top surface cleaner to do the job correctly without damaging the cooking surface. Cook top cleaner can be found in the cleaning supply section of your local grocery or hardware store.

If you have a stove with drip pans under the burners (electric) or under the grates (gas), these can be removed to be cleaned. Just gently pull them out, remove and wash the drip pans. If there is cooked on food, use a soft abrasive cleanser or baking soda, followed up with vinegar to easily remove baking soda residue.

You can also lift the front of the stove top for gas and electric stoves to get the food and crumbs which has fallen below the surface. Stove tops are usually just clicked into place. Gently lift the front of the stove top and it should click up and open for easy cleaning. Again, use a mild spray cleanser or abrasive and be sure you clean any residue before closing and replacing cleaned drip pans and cooking element or grate. Orange citrus spray cleansers are great for cutting grease and cleaning.

To clean an oven, first check to see if the oven is self-cleaning. If so, make sure you have wiped the inside down with a wet cloth and that you won't need the oven for about 12 hours and be prepared for the smell (baked in food burning away). When the timing is right, turn the oven to self-cleaning and begin. It will be done when it is done. The timer on the oven will set itself and will run down through the process.

Once you have begun the self-cleaning process, the oven will likely lock shut until it is complete. You will want to plan to be home to 'babysit' your oven during this time as it is doing its job the oven is essentially 'on' and should be attended as such. If your oven does not have a self-cleaning function, you may purchase oven cleaner spray in the cleaning supply section of the grocery/hardware store and follow the directions on the can carefully. Dress for cleaning and take care not to get any of these caustic cleaners on your skin. Wear gloves! Spray the entire inside surface of the oven. Let it sit and then scrub.

To ease you pain of cleaning an oven, protect the bottom of the oven with drip pans and/or aluminum foil and proper baking dishes when you are cooking in the oven.

Getting Social

Dressing the part, pulling it together and entertaining...let's throw a dinner party the right way!

Basic Guidelines for Dress Codes

Every event has a 'dress code'. Just like you would not wear an evening gown or tux with tails to a football game you would not wear your flip flops and 'team' shirt to your grandparents Golden Wedding Anniversary Party at their 'Club'. So always ask what the attire for the event is!

Formal means "Black Tie" - You may be familiar with the word "formal" but now it is also likely to be referred to as Black Tie. Men will need a suit or tuxedo. Whether you choose a suit or tuxedo is primarily based on the city in which the event occurs, along with the type of event. If an invitation reads, "Black Tie" and you want to impress…don't under-dress. Every man should own at least one two piece suit (not a swimsuit but matching slacks and jacket), preferably in dark navy, black or gray. Suits do go out of style and your suit size may change. Be sure you try it on and if need be, update your suit in time to make changes in advance of your event. If you choose to wear a tuxedo and don't own one…you can rent one. Tuxedo rental stores will help you with the accessories needed to create the prefect Black Tie look, which will include a bow tie. If you choose a suit, a white shirt, pressed, is best with a tie that suits your personality. The darker the tie, the more formal your look, especially if it is in a solid color. Always, always be sure your shoes are polished AND that the color of the shoes coordinates with the suit. Black shoes: grey, black, navy suit; brown shoes: brown or tan suit (tan suits are for summer season only).

Women: Evening gowns (not prom dresses) or little black dresses with something extra…enhance your look with sophisticated bling on your neck or ears; don't over-do it though. Let the neckline of your dress and the adornments of the dress guide your accessory choices.

And Semi-Formal now means "Black Tie" Optional: This leaves the level of "formal" up to you to a certain degree. Men: A tuxedo is acceptable, but most likely you would be most comfortable in dark suits with white dress shirt, solid color tie, which steps it up to a more formal look.

Women: This that 'little black dress' affair. Keep it classy, be sure it fits and always make sure you can walk in your shoes and the heels do not need new taps…that is tacky!

Just Exactly What is Business Casual? This may vary depending on the type of business you are associated with; go with what you would be expected to wear to the office. Unless you work at home in your bathrobe or at the beach in shorts, this means for men: khakis, slacks, polo shirt or button up and more casual shoes (which are still in good condition, match the pants, and are not athletic shoes or sandals) and that your clothes are pressed free of wrinkles and are clean.

Women: No shorts, flip flops, or inappropriately short skirts. If you are in the fashion business and jeans are acceptable, be sure they are the ones that do not need a trampoline to get into or the ones that have that "worn, ripped up look". Pair a great pair of jeans with a white fitted tee shirt or button up blouse and a fitted jacket with heels and you will be perfect…as long as jeans are acceptable for the situation.

Tying a Tie

1. Start with wide end of the tie on your right and extends a foot below the narrow end.

2. Cross wide end over the narrow end and bring up through the loop.

3. Cross wide end over the narrow end again and bring up through loop.

4. Then pull down through the loop and around across narrow as shown.

5. Turn and pass up through loop

6. Complete by slipping down through the knot in front. Tighten and draw up snug to collar.

Hosting a Dinner Party

Begin by deciding if you are having a themed party, casual barbeque or a more formal sit down dinner. Decide upon your guest list, keeping your budget in mind and then determine your meal. Send out written invitations, call, send E-vites (Email invitations) and get the word out to those you would like to entertain.

If you are providing the food, it is best to request RSVPs a day or two ahead of time. If you don't hear back from people, follow up so as not to waste your money and time on food that will not be eaten or could go bad if not used.

It is not uncommon to extend invitations with requests for guests to bring a dish of food for a potluck. It is up to you to assign categories to each guest, but remember if a guest flakes out at the last minute, that dish will not be part of your meal. If you are supplying the food, you may ask your guests to bring their favorite beverage and you can let them know the cuisine you will be serving if they want to compliment the meal.

If you want to go it alone and provide everything, plan out your menu, make a list of all the ingredients you will need to prepare each dish, take inventory of what you already have and then make your shopping list of needed items. Be sure you multiply the number of guests by the amount needed for each serving so you have enough food. You should factor in one or two extras for big eaters.

The same goes for beverages. Wine serves four glasses per bottle. Serve responsibly so you don't have someone leave your home in a condition non-conducive to driving. If your guest has over-indulged, have a sober driver take them home or make them a place to sleep. Do not allow your guests to risk their lives over a dinner party.

In addition to the table meal, will you be serving appetizers or snacks before the meal? These can be as easy as chips and dip along with fresh veggies for dipping. Or you can go all out and offer an array of yummy prepared starters from your favorite cookbook.

Make sure you have enough place settings of dishes, flatware and glasses for your guests. If you don't, borrow some or use disposables (great for a bbq, but not so much for a sit down dinner). It is the least stressful to prepare dishes you have already made in the past, so you know exactly how you expect them to come out and they taste good.

Simple things which can be made in advance and either heated up or refrigerated for serving will ease the work when your guests are at your party. Keep it simple with planning and preparation. You should be having as much fun as your guests.

Let your guests help if you need, before, during and don't forget clean up. There is nothing that ruins a good evening more than waking up to a house that looks like it's been ransacked. It is common courtesy to help, so if you are the guest, offer to help even if your offer is declined, you won't look like the ungrateful visitor.

Introducing People

Whether in your own home, at a social function or in a business setting there is nothing more awkward than not being introduced. Many times we may forget the name of the person we have come upon and the person we are with is left standing looking lost or left out. If I have not been introduced within the first couple of minutes I will put my friend/colleague at ease and extend my hand introducing myself. Your friend may have forgotten the other persons name or they may not have manners. Whatever the case, I am not invisible.

Guidelines for introductions:

In business situations, use both first and last names when appropriate and known along with how that person and you are affiliated. The higher ranking would be introduced first. Ex:: "Mr. Smith, this is Suzanne Williams, she is a new associate with the firm?

When introducing people, it's nice to say "I'd like you to meet…" or "this is my friend, boss, sister …. And this is….."

The elder person is introduced to the younger…"Grandma, this is my boyfriend, John" "John, this is my Grandma, Mrs. Smith, but she likes to be called Anne"

Always extend your hand and greet your new introduction with a firm handshake whether you are a man or woman. Not so firm that they walk away having to see the hand surgeon. No one likes to shake hands with a limp, lifeless hand. Exude confidence with your handshake.

Setting a Table Properly

How many guests will you be having at your sit down meal? Do you have enough place settings of dishes, flatware and glasses?

If you are going to use a tablecloth you will need a pad underneath to keep it place. The tablecloth should hang down about 18" around the table for the proper fit. If you are buying one, know the size of your table before you head out.

- At each chair, place a plate with a folded napkin in the center of the plate

- Place the dinner fork (large fork) to the left of the plate and the salad fork (smaller) to the left of the dinner fork. Place the larger fork nearest the plate.

- Place a knife to the right of the plate, with the cutting edge toward the plate. For chicken or a game bird, you might want to add a steak knife.

- Put out two spoons if you're serving soup and a dessert which requires a spoon. The small dessert spoon is placed to the right of the knife and the larger, deeper, more rounded soup spoon is to the right of the dessert spoon. If you wish, you can wait on the dessert spoons until after the main course is completed.

- Place a bread plate with a (small) butter knife (if you have them) just above the forks on the left.

- Beverage glasses are placed to the right of the plate above the spoon/knives.

These guidelines are for a more formal, full course meal. If you are dining more casually, you can forego many of the utensils and just stick with fork, knife and spoon and your guests can use the same fork for their salad and meal. If you are serving meat which requires a sharper edge, you may need a regular knife and a steak knife.

Tipping/Gratuities

Gratuity, commonly referred to as tipping, is money given to service providers for their service. While gratuity has become expected and if you are a service provider, you know how much of a difference it can make in your income if you are stiffed; a tip is still at the discretion of you as the customer. TIP stands for "to insure professionalism," if you do not receive good service then a tip does not need to be given. If you do receive adequate service, the following guidelines are standard in most states:

- Restaurant and bar services: 15% for good service, 20% for exceptional, cocktail server or bartender, 15-20% or $1 per drink.

- Hotel Bellmen, Airport Curbside Bellmen: $1-2 per bag.

- Hotel room housekeepers: $5-10 per night.

- Car Parking Valet: $2-$5.

- Hair stylists and skin care professionals: 15-20% per service provider.

- Taxi Driver 10-15% of total fare

- Room Service Delivery 15% of the bill (be sure it is not already included in room service fee)

- Pizza Delivery 10% of bill

- Hair Stylist/Barber/Skin Care Therapist/Massage Therapist

Gift Buying and Card Sending

Questions to ask yourself when considering a gift purchase:

- Who is the gift for?

- What are their interests?

- What is their favorite color?

- How much money do I have to spend?

- If I am mailing the gift, how large of an item am I prepared to spend money shipping?

- Would a gift certificate or card be easier with just as much impact

- Is there something I can order online and have shipped directly?

- Can I make a gift that is more personal and will show my genuine effort and heartfelt love?

Gifts can be tricky, but what's most important to remember is that when you are giving a gift, who is the recipient and what do they like? Have you ever received a gift and thought to yourself, "What the heck were they thinking…they are into comics, not me." Don't buy something you like for someone you aren't sure enjoys the same things.

Think about your recipient, does your Mom or girlfriend really want the newest video game? Does your Dad or boyfriend really want a cookbook or "Chick Flick"? Sometimes a heartfelt card or hand written letter is the best gift a person can receive, don't believe a gift's value is in the price tag. Some things are priceless.

Holiday Dates

New Year's Day- January 1

Martin Luther King, Jr. Day 3rd Monday of January

Valentine's Day February 14

Presidents Day 3rd Monday of February

Easter Sunday changes each year usually between Mar. 22 & April 25

Passover changes each year

Mother's Day (2nd Sunday of May)

Memorial Day (last Monday of May, traditionally 30 May)

Father's Day (3rd Sunday of June)

Independence Day – July 4

Labor Day (first Monday of September)

Rosh Hashanah and Yom Kippur changes each year

Halloween- October 31

Veterans Day-11 November 11

Thanksgiving (4th Thursday of November)

Christmas Day- December 25

New Year's Eve-December 31

For holidays that change each year based on different calendars, search the web for the holiday and you will find the exact date for each year.

Remember who gave you life and never, ever forget their birthday.

Greenbacks or Plastic?

Knowing your budget, how to save money, how to qualify for credit and housing is a necessity. Don't go broke and don't let someone else spend your money if you lose your debit card. Know how to plan, protect yourself and stay in good standing.

Applying for a Job

Finding a job can be an arduous task but a necessary chore if you are going to support yourself in part or in full. Steps to take before you begin your search so you have clarity with what you want and get what you set out to find are…Write down:

- What you enjoy doing

- How much money do you need to earn?

- How many work hours are you seeking?

- What are the hours you are available to work?

- What date are you available to start?

- What is a reasonable commute to your job from school or home?

- What skills do you have and what are you qualified to do?

- Are there any certifications or training you can get that will increase your ability to get hired?

- Put together a current resume, include volunteer positions if they are relevant to what you are seeking

When you have compiled your answers, it should read something like this:

I enjoy (ex: taking care of children, cooking, cleaning, graphic design, sales, marketing etc.). I need to earn no less than $15 per hour. I am available to work 25 hours per week, Monday through Sunday from 10-7. I am available to begin my new job on (date), my job needs to be within 15 minutes driving distance from my home. I have experience as a babysitter, I have worked at a local restaurant, I was editor of the school newspaper, manager of the student store, I sold fundraising products while in school, I washed cars, mowed lawns, I volunteered at my church in the office or daycare, I am a trained barista, I helped at my parent's business cleaning after hours, I fluently speak a second language, I have tutored younger kids in English, Spanish, math.

I could be more valuable if I had my CPR certification which I can get through my local fire department. I would be a more viable candidate if I had my food handler's card. My references will be stronger with letters of recommendation from previous employers or organization leaders I have worked with, paid or not.

Now use this information along with your name, address, phone number and email address to put together a simple resume which will expedite the application process in many cases. There will still be applications to fill out, but you will have all of the information with you when you are searching.

After you have clarity on what type of position you are seeking, begin your search by checking:

- Job boards or listings through your school.

- Ask friends or your parents friends if they have any leads.

- Check online at Craigslist.com or your local classified advertisement pages.

Get out and hit the pavement…even if you don't see a sign in the window, if a business is enticing to you, go in and ask if they are currently or will be hiring in the near future and ask to leave a resume or fill out an application.

Get business cards printed up if you have services you would like to offer on your own. Vistaprint.com is a very inexpensive online way to get professional looking business cards quickly. If you are going to offer your own services, be sure you have a business license and any other licenses or insurance to present yourself as a professional and to comply with local and state laws and the Internal Revenue Service. You can't forget that you have to pay taxes as an adult.

Once you have secured interviews, be sure you know the name of the person interviewing you and arrive early. Do not over inflate your job qualifications; it will backfire in your face.

Always send a thank you card after the interview. A great idea is to have the card with you, stamped and ready to fill in so you can leave the interview, stop outside or in your car, complete it and drop it in the mail.

You want to set yourself apart from other candidates based on first impressions. That thank you note arriving in the mail a day or two after the interview will continue to help you make an impression on the person responsible for filling the position. Thank them for their consideration of you as a team member to their organization and the time they have given you to learn more about the position. Sign the note legibly so they know who it came from. Keep it short and simple.

Believe in yourself; don't settle on just any job unless you are in dire straits. Do what you love so you don't hate your job. Earn money and support yourself financially with a smile and a sense of satisfaction.

Lost/Stolen Card or Checkbook

The most important thing to know if you find you have lost your credit/debit card is the card number and the lost/stolen card phone number to call. Keep these numbers somewhere that you can access them in the event of this misfortune. Not in your wallet along with the cards, in case the entire wallet or purse disappears.

If you have a card through your bank, you can usually call the bank and they can look up your account information with your social security number and by answering your security questions. This is just a slower way than calling the direct number with the accurate information.

If you feel you may have just misplaced the card and don't want to cancel it, many institutions will allow you to put a hold on usage of the card for a couple of days. This is the best way to protect yourself while you search. With so many purchases made today with a swipe of a card and no person checking for a signature, you can really get into trouble if your card lands in the hands of a dishonest person. If you are sure it has been stolen, cancel it immediately.

Difference between a Debit Card and a Credit Card

Debit cards can often be used as credit cards, without a signature if there is a visa/master card symbol on the front. This is especially important because it means the card can be used without a pin or security code if it is stolen. A debit card looks like a credit card, but the money must be in the account it is attached to for it to work. It may also be referred to as a check card.

A credit card is a revolving charge account, it has a limit and it has an interest rate; it usually costs you money to use it. It also has severe charges if you pay your bill late or go over your limit. If you have a credit card, remember this is money that must be paid back in a timely and scheduled manner. Your repayment record is recorded with the credit reporting agencies and how you handle your payments will either enhance your score or could ruin your credit.

Don't get into credit trouble. Don't use a credit card if you cannot afford to make the payments. A credit card is a good way to establish a good credit rating, just be careful, and read all of the fine print before you sign up and understand and agree to their terms.

Budgeting

This book is not meant to teach all of the fundamentals of life and therefore, is not going into a lot of details about the financial aspects of your life. There are experts out there with books and tools specifically designed to teach you how to handle money. That said, here is a simple guide to not overspending and/or budgeting: Know how much money you earn or are given for monthly expenses, then make a list of what you can afford for you living expenses. How do they balance? If you would be spending more than your income, you need to make more money or cut some of your expenditures. It's really that simple, make more or cut things out. Do not use credit or "payday" loans as a solution to financial short comings. You will find yourself in a world of trouble for a long time if you abuse credit cards and loans.

Having good credit can take you a long way when you need it, so protect your credit rating. Pay on time, don't over use, don't pay late and don't have more credit cards than you need. It is good to establish one or two credit cards, use them and pay them off. This shows creditors that you are responsible and reliable, which is factored in if you apply for a loan from a bank for a car, home or perhaps even a business.

Opening a Checking Account

If this is your first time to open a checking account, it might be a good idea to ask your parents or friends who they use for their banking and why they have chosen that institution. Once you have decided on one or more institutions to consider, you will want to call or stop by and ask about the checking accounts they offer.

Many banks offer "free" checking, but ask what that really means. Some topics to cover are overdraft protection and debit card usage:

- Is it free for a certain period of time?

- What are the requirements for "free"? Does free include free checks?

- Do you need to keep a certain amount of money in for a minimum amount of time?

- Is there overdraft protection and what are the overdraft charges?

- Does free include a debit card?

- Are there fees associated with debit card usage?

Many of these answers may be found online, but it is always best to speak to a human to be sure you are clear on the policies associated with the account that works best for you. In order to actually open an account, you will have to go to the bank in person and you will need to be sure you are prepared by bringing photo identification.

Credit Rating

Your credit rating is which gives creditors, lenders, and landlords a reference to your likely credit worthiness based upon your ability to repay a loan or credit card. Determining factors are your debt to income ration, how much you owe compared to what you earn. What is the payment history of previous debts? This number is attached you is determined by your payment history and number of accounts opened.

There are three credit bureaus, Experian, Equifax, and TransUnion which compile information about your credit worthiness with information provided to them by previous debtors.

While in the past, your credit or FICO score, a three digit number was used primarily for getting a credit card or loan, now your credit score may be used to determine employment eligibility, deposits on loans or utilities and even insurance premiums.

So your credit score is more important to your future than just the ability to borrow money, which is why it is so important to protect with timely payments, paying more than the minimums each month, and not maxing out your credit limits. You also want to establish credit; no credit is many times as detrimental as bad credit. As soon as you are of legal adult age, 18 years old in the United States, apply for a credit card with a low spending limit. Use it and pay it off; this is a way to build your credit.

Be advised that your credit rating will be affected by frequent inquiries. You are not penalized for checking your own credit rating, once a year. But your credit score will lower a few points when other loan agencies check it. So don't go shopping for a car and have every lot you stop at run your credit. You must authorize a credit report run on you, be cautious.

To check your own credit, you can go online to one of the three reporting agencies or search credit ratings. There are many online services which will, for a fee, allow you to check your rating regularly, offer advice to build or repair your credit and monitor reportings. Look for something that best suits your needs and their pricing before signing up. Most of these online services do not have an easy opt-out; you will need to call to cancel. Know what you are getting yourself into before you sign up.

When Life Serves You Lemons

Emergencies are not planned events! You don't usually get an opportunity after the fact to let people know what you want or need them to do if you are caught in an emergency situation. Don't wait until it is too late; do you want to wind up without anyone knowing who they should call if you can't speak for yourself? Take care of yourself and those who love you. You need to know when you need them.

First Aid Kit Essentials

Keep a replenished first kit in your home at all times, where it is easy to get to, either in the linen closet or in the kitchen cabinet under the sink. You can purchase prepared first aid kits at a drug store or at Costco or you can put your own together. I find it easier and more cost effective to purchase an assembled kit for under $30. Your kit should include:

- Antibiotic ointment

- Aspirin and Ibuprofen

- Alcohol cleaning pads

- Antiseptic wipes

- Several different sized adhesive bandages

- Sterile Latex free gloves

- Tweezers

- Cotton tipped swabs

- Gauze pads in a couple of sizes

- First aid tape

- An instant cold compress

- Finger splint

- Butterfly wound adhesive closures

- Ace Bandage for wrapping a sprain

- First Aid Reference Guide

- Medium sized safety pins

- Sterile eye pad

This is also a good place to keep a listing of your doctor's contact information. Numbers for hospital, poison control center and of course, in an emergency dial 911 first!

Things you should keep in your Wallet or Purse

Your identification, a $20 bill, four quarters for a pay phone, your emergency contact information, your medical insurance card, a condom (be advised that condoms breakdown when kept in a wallet for too long and they also have expiration dates…if the wrapper is looking worn, it's probably risky protection).

Doctor's Name and Phone Number

Keep this number along with that of your dentist with your emergency contact numbers; on your fridge or a cabinet that is visible to all. Your doctor should have records on file that could be critical to your care in case of an unexpected medical emergency. That means these numbers should be in your wallet and in a visible safe place in your home, in case someone else is calling on your behalf. This information may also be needed for insurance coverage purposes. It's not a bad idea to have a copy of your insurance card alongside the medical contacts and numbers.

Grease Burns

Rinse the area that has been splattered under cool water, if the skin is broken, seek medical attention. If it is not, and feels like bad sunburn, treat the area by applying aloe vera gel to cool and calm. If blisters appear, keep the area clean and dry. If they do not go away seek medical attention as this could be a more serious burn.

Overflowing Toilet

Reach behind the toilet and turn the knob coming out from the wall all the way to the right immediately. ("Lefty loosey, righty tighty" - to loosen turn to the right and to tighten turn to the left).

A Clogged Toilet

Allow the water which is in the bowl to slowing drain down enough so that you can safely plunge without pushing water over the edges of the toilet. Take a plunger and clear whatever is clogging the toilet causing it to overflow. To use the plunger, insert the rubber suction cup or bell into the toilet bowl creating a seal between the rubber plunger head and the toilet bowl. When there is enough room in the bowl to insert the plunger without overflowing, flush the toilet and plunge simultaneously.

If with regular usage the bowl continues to plug, it is possible that something which doesn't belong in the toilet was accidentally dropped in and is clogging the regular flow, which would require an expensive plumber. Keep all things that could cause this to happen off of the top of the back of the toilet such as toothbrushes, small combs, hair ties. Don't flush items that are not meant to be flushed either; this includes feminine hygiene products or condoms.

When you have cleared the blockage, shake the dirty plunger off in the toilet and with toilet paper or a paper towel under it, transfer it to the tub or shower to rinse it off in hot, hot water.

A Running Toilet

Wiggle the handle, if the problem persists, a part in the tank may need to be replaced. You will either have to call the landlord or a plumber. A running toilet is wasting water and if you are paying the water bill, it will annoy your bank account as much as the sound of running water is annoying you.

Sometimes the flapper inside the back bottom tank of the toilet just needs to be adjusted (easy) or replaced (call the landlord). Remove the ceramic toilet lid on the tank to check it out. It is also possible that the chain that raises and lowers the flapper may have gotten caught or fallen off the handle.

Circuit Breaker

When you move into your house or apartment, ask the landlord or your roommate to show you where the breaker box is located. When a fuse has blown or a circuit has been overloaded it will usually flip out of position. Many breaker boxes have been labeled to indicate the rooms or appliances they are supplying power to. This will also help you determine which breaker has "flipped".

Be sure power is turned off to light switches and power appliances are turned off or unplugged. Go to the box and reset the switch by turning it completely off and then set it back to the on position. Switched to the left is generally ON. Then make sure you don't overload again by powering on all of the same items which caused the fuse to blow in the first place.

If the switch does not remain on or does not turn the power back on, contact your landlord as the fuse may need to be replaced by a professional. WARNING: Never replace a fuse yourself.

Who to call if...

Important Numbers to keep handy:

_____

_____

_____

_____

_____

_____

_____

_____

_____

_____

_____

_____

_____

Your Landline Telephone isn't Working

Call the phone company you have set up your landline service with for landlines and/or internet service using your cell phone. The number should be on any bill. If your cell phone is out and you have no landline, ask to use a neighbor's or friend's phone.

The Power goes Out

Call the electric or gas company; the number is on your bill!

The Cable goes Out

Call the cable company; check your bill for the number.

There is a Medical Emergency

DIAL 911 first!

You smell Smoke or Gas at your House

FIRST get out of the house immediately and DIAL 911, move away from the structure and wait for emergency crews to arrive and locate the source. Do not stay in a dwelling where there are toxic fumes or fire. Be sure you yell to let others know to get out!

You Feel an Intruder is Trying to Get into Your House

DIAL 911 and lock the door of the room you are in.

Questions about my Schooling and Scheduling

Call the school counseling office and speak to your assigned counselor, advisor or their assistant.

If I need to Call in Sick to Work

Call your employer with as much advance notice as possible and follow company policy for calling in sick. Is it your responsibility to find someone to cover your shift? If so, be sure you have the list of names and numbers to get the shift covered.

If I need a Hair Cut

Ask friend or colleagues for referrals unless you want to risk having Edward ScissorHands take a wack at your mane. It's also a good idea to have an idea in mind when you make your appointment of what you would like the outcome to be. It never hurts to take a picture in with you to show the stylist but remember, you are not the person in the picture nor is the person doing your hair the same person who did the picture. Don't expect to walk out looking exactly like the picture. And take heed to the advise of the stylist if they tell you that style or color will not be flattery to you. They want you to leave looking your best if it is a reputable salon seeking your return business.

If I get Sick and I don't have a Doctor

Look for a walk-in clinic, but note that they may require payment up front if you do not have insurance coverage. Options for payment usually include credit cards.

If I need to see the Dentist

Ask friends who they use and get a referral.

The Dog ate Chocolate

Call a veterinarian immediately. They will ask you type and size of dog and the quantity of chocolate consumed by your dog. This is critical information for the treatment of your pet. Chocolate can be deadly to dogs, it is not a cute treat.

Can't Drive a Broken Car

If you don't want to pay for the expensive tow service and you haven't realized the importance of a road side assistance plan, then you better know how to take care of the details to keep your car on the road and off the road if it breaks down.

Changing a Tire

Tools you need:

- Spare Tire

- Lug Nut Wrench

- Jack

- Flashlight

- Flare or Caution Reflective cone or sign

If you feel like you have had a blow out or your tire has just gone flat, pull as far off to the side of the road as possible in a well-lighted, flat area. Turn the car off, set the parking break, and turn on your emergency flashers/hazard lights. Check to see if there is enough air to get to the nearest gas station or tire repair store. If not, prepare to change a tire. Set out flares behind the vehicle to alert other drivers if it is dark or bad weather or you are on a major highway.

Get the spare tire and tools from the trunk, your spare tire may be hidden under the mat in the trunk, lift it up and loosen the center wing nut to remove the tire. It is likely to be smaller than the tire you are removing. If it is a smaller, temporary tire, be sure you get a full sized tire to replace it as soon as possible.

Place the tire on the ground near the flat tire along with your lug nut wrench (a wrench that is shaped like an addition sign which is made specifically to fit the nuts which hold the tire onto the frame of the car), your car jack, and a flash light if it is dark.

Use the sharp flat end of the lug nut wrench or jack handle to pop the hubcap off of the center of the tire/wheel to expose the lug nuts that hold the tire to the wheel. Using the lug nut wrench, before the car has been jacked up, loosen the lug nuts that are holding the wheel in place. You only need to loosen them about a ½ turn clockwise. You do not want to take them off, just getting them started before the car is lifted. You don't want the tire to fall off while it is being jacked up.

Check your vehicle's owner's manual to find the safest correct place for installing the jack under the car. Once the jack is installed lift the car up using a crank that is with the jack. Lift the car up high enough to remove the flat tire and slide the fully inflated tire in its place.

When the car is high enough, finish removing the lug nuts from the flat tire. Do not lose lug nuts; keep them together close at hand. Take the flat tire off, then lift and place the good tire on the exposed lug bolts. Align the holes on the tire and slide into place with the air valve of the tiring facing outward.

Put the lug nuts back on first finger tight with wrench. Tighten nuts opposite one another to set the tire, and then continue tightening all nuts around in a star pattern. Tighten only "fast" and not tight until the next step, you are just keeping the tire straight on the wheel at this point.

Slowly lower the vehicle to the ground using the jack. Once the tire is on the ground, tighten the lug nuts as tightly as possible.

Car Breaks Down on the Side of the Road

Try to get your vehicle to a brightly lit area if it is dark. Pull as far off of the road out of the way of traffic as possible. Activate your emergency flashers. Use your cell phone to call for assistance; if you are in a new area without many friends or family, it is a good idea to have a roadside assistance plan whether it is AAA (American Automobile Association) or another assistance service.

If your car temperature gauge goes into the red zone and your car is hot, do not get out and put the hood up and try to open the radiator cap if your car is overheating; it will likely explode in your face. An overheated car turned into 2nd degree burns on my sister's face resulting in an unplanned facial chemical peel.

Things You Should Always Have in Your Car

In the trunk:

- jacket

- blanket

- spare tire and tire jack

- gallon of water

- some energy food bars

- walking shoes

- flares

- jumper cables

- gas can

- first aid kit

In the Glove Box:

- Emergency phone numbers

- Car cell phone charger

- Auto manual

- Verification of valid insurance coverage

- Your automobile registration.

Checking the Oil in Your Car

Following the guidelines in the car's owner manual is your true guide to getting this important task completed. It is not a bad idea to make this a monthly routine if you know your vehicle is not obviously leaking oil.

If you see oil spots where you routinely park, you should check the oil more often and get the car to a mechanic to find out why it is leaking. If you run a vehicle without oil, you will burn up the engine and your car will be toast…and I mean burnt toast with thousands of dollars for repairs.

Using the manual, find out where your oil dipstick is located; this is the measuring stick which is a slim long metal wand that measures the oil in your car's engine. It usually has a small ring on the top for you to pull up on and pull it out of the vessel. Once found, pull it out with the vehicle turned off and wipe it clean with a rag or paper towel. Reinsert and pull out again, this will show the level of oil in the vessel. There will be slash mark indicators on the dipstick which the oil mark should fall between.

If it is low, follow the instruction in the owner's manual indicating the best weight of oil for your car. You can purchase oil at a gas station, variety store or hardware store. If you car is not below the line but near it you can add some oil but take care not to overfill your oil reservoir. Add oil a bit at a time, then re-measure, following measurement guidelines until your levels are within the indication markings on the dipstick. You can keep the extra, if you have any, in your trunk or in your garage or other safe, dry storage place.

Buying Car Insurance

The Geico commercials you see on television are no joke. Go on the internet and do your research. You will need to know the make, model and year of the vehicle you are searching to get insurance coverage on, along with knowledge of your driving history. You will be asked if you have a clean driving record or if you have accidents and tickets. These things will be factored into pricing, along with your age and that of your vehicle for determining the estimated monthly/annual cost of insurance premiums.

Gap Coverage, do you have it? If you are driving a car with a loan on it, you better make sure you do. Gap coverage comes into play if you have purchased a car with a loan and your car is damaged beyond the value of the car which could be less than you actually owe. Gap coverage will pay off the loan so you don't have to pay out of pocket for the difference between value and amount owed. Ask your agent.

Checking the Pressure in your Car Tires

Tire gauges are tools that are used to measure the pressure in your tires. Tires are meant to be driven at specific air pressure for best performance, longer lasting tires and best gas mileage from your vehicle. Tire gauges can be purchased at automotive repair stores and often at hardware and or variety stores. It is a good idea to keep this tool in your car if you want to be diligent about your tire pressure.

You may visibly be able to tell that your tire pressure is low if one tire appears to be lower than the rest. Get to a service station where there is an air compressor to fill up the tire. The air hose will often have a gauge on the end which will measure the amount of air in the tire and how much you are putting in.

There is no standard for how much air is in every tire, they all vary. Air in tires is measured in lbs (pounds), and is usually indicated on the side of the tire. If you don't see it there, check your vehicle owner's manual for guidelines. Failure to keep your car's tires filled to the indicated levels can lead to the tires wearing out quicker or if they are overfilled, cause damage and dangerous consequences.

Jump Starting a Car

If a car will not start when the key is turned in the ignition, the first thing to check is the battery. You can do this by looking to see if the interior lights come on. When the key is in the auxiliary position does the radio come on? If these things are not working, it's time to give your car a jump start.

You need a pair of jumper cables and another operational vehicle; you also need to know where the battery is located in your vehicle (under the front hood or in the trunk is where you will usually find it). The working car needs to pull up so the location of their battery is within a reasonable distance to your battery to connect the cables, but not touching your vehicle (this is important!).

Once the cars are in position, you will take the plastic caps off the battery posts so they are exposed, be sure to notice which one is positive (or marked with a "+") and which one is negative (-). The cable clamps are generally marked black for negative and red for positive. Clamp the red or positive cable clamp to the positive post on the operational vehicle battery and then the negative or black clamp to the negative post. Then connect the positive or red clamp to the corresponding post on the dead battery and then the black to the negative.

Once you are sure that positive is connected to positive on both ends of cables and negative to negative, you start the ignition on the operational vehicle. This sends energy to the dead battery. Let the operational vehicle run for a few minutes, giving it gas to "rev" up the rpms of the engine and then try to start the car with the dead battery. It may crank right up or it may take a few minutes of charging depending on how dead the battery is. Once you get the car with the dead battery started, you will want to make sure you keep the car running and maybe even drive around the block to charge the battery before you shut the vehicle off again.

Extreme cold weather, leaving lights on and not driving frequently are things that will deplete the battery. So even if you don't use your car for regular transportation, it is important to at least start it once a week to keep the battery charged.

If your battery seems to be "dying" regularly for no apparent reason, go to a local mechanic and they should be able to tell you if the battery needs to be replaced (they should test your battery for no charge).

There could be another problem such as the battery posts are corroded. You can scrub the corrosion off with a wire brush (wire barbeque grill cleaning brush will do in a pinch), the battery cables could be loose or corroded and need to be replaced, the alternator may be going bad if the car is not starting once you have tried jump starting or the battery could just need to be replaced.

Batteries have lives and are dated, check the date on your battery. If it is five years old or more, you will likely need to replace it. It's easiest if you take the old battery with you, so you can be sure you are purchasing the correct replacement. Most places that sell batteries also will take care of proper disposal of the old one.

Odds and Ends

What do I do if my PC freezes up?

Reboot it, press and hold down the power button or control, alt, delete keys at the same time if your computer is a PC...90% of computer problems can be solved with a hard reboot. This is done as above if the computer is not allowing you to turn it off and restart with the normal process. Your computer should be turned off (rebooted) at least once a week to keep the speed of the computer running efficiently.

What happens if my PC crashes?

Back up your computer at least once a week to an external hard drive which can be purchased for about $100. This could be the best $100 you will ever spend.

What if you spill liquid on the keyboard?

Replace the keyboard. If you spill liquid on your laptop keyboard, you will likely need to replace the laptop. Turn the keyboard or laptop over quickly to drain as much of the liquid off as possible and let it air dry. You can speed up this process by turning on a room fan and let it blow across the keyboard or using a hair blow dryer on lowest heat setting. If the keyboard does not function after it is dry, call an expert.

Mailing a Package

The easiest thing to do is reference the websites of your preferred shipping service. The websites are easy to navigate and will answer many of your questions, as well as give you their specific guidelines on what they will or won't ship, how things should be packed for proper shipping, their size and weight restrictions and fees.

United States Postal Service   www.usps.com

Federal Express   www.fedex.com

UPS   www.ups.com

Make Sure You Have a Hard Copy of Phone Numbers

Many phones now have the ability to sync your phone with your computer contact lists. This is great in the case that you lose your phone. Be aware though, with an Iphone, it has been experienced that if your phone is not synced and stored to your outlook contact file or other data list and you update your phone, you may lose all of the contacts from your phone or pieced together incorrectly. So always sync before updating with an Iphone.

Removing Stains from Carpet

Blot any excess moisture from the stain that you can, this is always the first step! Don't rub it; take a paper towel and blot, blot, blot. Keep using additional towels until you have absorbed as much of the liquid from the spill as possible. Don't soak or wipe it, otherwise you will set the stain for life. Know your stain. Figure out what kind of stain you have first. Unlike clothing, carpet stains can often be difficult to discern after a few moments. Smell it if you have to, seriously, sometimes that is the only way to know what created that particular stain.

For grease stains: Dab with a small amount of dry-cleaning fluid (found at a variety store, grocery or home store like Ace Hardware).

Then, blot with a small amount (pea-sized) of dishwashing liquid mixed with a cup or so of warm water. Blot from the outside edges of stain moving in toward center, and let stand for five minutes.

For juices and wines: Mix a small amount of laundry detergent with lukewarm water (or ammonia) and blot the stain. Then, sponge lightly with club soda and blot with the detergent-water solution again.

For egg and dairy products: Blot with ammonia and sponge with warm water. Then, blot with white vinegar and warm-water mixture using a fresh sponge or clean white cloth.

For ink: Blot with dry-cleaning fluid, and then use a small amount of laundry detergent (again, pea-sized mixed with a cup or so of lukewarm water (or ammonia, about a teaspoon) and blot stain from outside of stain to center, place towels over the stain and let dry, overnight if needed.

This is a universal step that should be done whenever you have removed a stain: Cover cleaned stain area with a clean white towel or cloth and let dry. Brush area clean and vacuum after the cleaned area is dry. The flat brush should pick up any dried particles that linger, and the vacuum will do the rest.

Using a Payphone

This may seem like an archaic suggestion and you may even be wondering if there are still such antiquities to use…the answer is yes, they may just be few and far between and even difficult to find. However, if you are in a jam, have lost your cell phone, are out of range or in a compromising situation and need to call someone, you should know how to use one.

Pay phones can be engaged with money or with a prepaid phone card. At this time, most pay phones require at least two quarters for each call. Calls are usually for a limited amount of time and require more money for more minutes. Long distance calling can be quite expensive on a payphone unless you make a collect call.

Prepaid phone cards can be purchased at supermarkets, variety stores, and convenience stores. They allow you to purchase a number of minutes and if you shop around, you will find that there can be a big discrepancy in the amount charged per minute. Obviously you want the best deal, so do compare pricing. Also, be advised that most of the cards will also reduce your balance with each call made, even if you do not make a connection. This is just a usage fee. So, either keep some change on you or a phone card in case of an emergency; you never know when you might need it so be prepared!

Starting a Lawn Mower

First determine the type of machine you have: electric machine or a gas mower. To start an electric model, attach the power cord to a long extension cord and plug it in, then turn the mower "on". If it is a gas mower, fill the proper tank with gasoline from a gas can. Usually you must also prime the tank by pushing a little button near where you poured in the gas. When you have done this, you will likely hold the throttle in or the bar across the top of the handle to keep the lawnmower in the idle position and pull the cord. It may take a couple of pulls, but the engine should get started. You may have to prime the motor more than once.

If it doesn't start after several attempts there could be something else wrong. Most gas motors usually need to have oil as well, so be sure to check this. If you have purchased a new mower, it should come with a manual. If you purchase one which is used, ask the person you are buying it from to show you how it starts. This will ensure that it works before you buy it and you will know how to start it when you begin using it.

A lawn mower is a great way to keep your own yard looking presentable, but also to earn extra money. Many people have raised families doing yard work and landscape maintenance. You can put money in your bank account while going to school by doing the same thing.

Starting a Fire in a Fireplace

To begin with, do you have a gas, electric or wood burning fireplace? If you have a gas fireplace, you will have an outside source of fuel which will need to be filled and checked regularly by the gas or propane company.

The pilot light should be lit by the company providing the service and you will have a small flame, which is your pilot. This will always be burning as long as there is gas in the tank. If your pilot light goes out, be sure to contact the company or landlord. You want to be sure that you are safe and are not putting a flame to an unknown fuel source which could cause an explosion.

A gas fireplace is usually easily ignited, started with the flip of a switch located near the side of the fireplace. There is also a gas valve usually found to one side of the fireplace. If the flames go out, use the tool (if needed) to turn the valve off. This will shut off the gas coming into the fireplace and give you time to safely call the company or landlord.

An electric fireplace is usually a "fake" flame. It will give you a glow without an actual flame and because it is electric, there will be a switch. Turn it on and off as you want to enjoy the ambiance. Never leave it on when leaving the building or going to bed.

If you have a wood burning fireplace, first be sure the flue is open, so that when you begin building your fire the smoke goes up the chimney and not in your house.

Your fire will burn easiest with dry smaller pieces of wood, not a huge thick log. The easiest and quickest way to get a fire started is by using a fire starter log which can be purchased at the store. This is a log that has chemicals and formed sawdust which is encased in a paper wrapping. Place this beneath your stacked wood, which should be stacked in the shape of a teepee, ends up. If you want to avoid the starter log, place crumbled up newspaper in the center of your teepee and light the paper on fire. This should get a good fire going. Another alternative is to buy and use Duraflame logs which are again, preformed and wrapped logs.

You always want to be sure that toxic fumes are not filling your home and causing sickness, which could be deadly. Always be sure, no matter the nature of your flame, that you have windows open an inch or so for ventilation. Fires burn oxygen and emit carbon monoxide which is a deadly, silent, odorless poison. It is critical that your home has smoke and carbon monoxide poison detectors to alert you to the build-up of these gases or too much smoke which could be deadly. Be sure to test your smoke and carbon monoxide detectors each month to be sure the batteries are good.

A to Z Different Uses for Things Around the House

Ankle Weight - Use as a door stop

Broom – Sweep away cobwebs from ceilings and corners

CDs – Use old CDs as coasters for glasses

Dryer Sheet – Slip a couple in stinky shoes in the closet

Eyeglass/Sunglass Case – Store tweezers, nail clippers

Frames from old pictures – Use as a serving tray

Grater – Strain seeds from hand squeezed citrus juice

Hydrogen Peroxide – Dipped cotton swab cleans key board

Ironing Board – Doubles as serving station for party with cover

Jewel CD Case – Use as a windshield ice scraper n the winter

Knife – Slip into hem of table cloth/both sides to hold down

Lemon- Removes stains and odors from cutting board

Matchbook – Use the strike strip to smooth jagged finger nail

Newspaper Bag   Store a wet umbrella

Olive Oil – Rub on snaggy, dry cuticles

Paper Clip – Replace a lost zipper pull on a hoodie

Quarter Coin – Measure things, it's almost one inch diameter

Rice – Cleans coffee grinder when ground and then wiped out

Scissors – Cut up pizza if you don't have a pizza slicer

Twist Tie – Tie together tangled window shade cords

Underwear – Old t shirts make great cleaning rags

Vinegar – Remove coffee/tea stain from a cup, swish then wash

Wine Bottle – Keep your "boots" in shape, slip a bottle in them

Xtra Magazines – Make a vision board of your dreams…cut phrases and pictures and paste on a poster board, use this to visualize all that you want in your life! Use magazine, newspapers, personal pictures…whatever you want, things, circumstances, success!

Yoga Mat – Line cabinets for cushion glass storage

Ziplock Baggies – Store opened bean, rice, pasta for freshness

Conclusion

Starting out on your own can be a bit intimidating but hopefully the ideas, directions, and resources contained in this book will help make you feel not only confident but capable of making a go of it! While the ideas and directions contained in this book are intended to give you a push and a prod in the right direction they are in no way complete.

It is hoped that this book is useful to anyone on their own for the first time and facing the realities of life with insurance, budgets, and bills and the responsibilities that go with them. Use this book as a reference guide and navigational tool over and over. Don't memorize the contents of this book because your focus should be on the really important things in your life like your career and family. Instead leave it out where you can have ready access for the things that pop up and need to be resolved along the way.

We all learn reading, writing, and arithmetic in school but no one teaches us how to find a roommate, open a bank account, or check the oil in the car. Now you know how!

Hopefully you are aware of practical effective ways to solve some of the things that you face as you venture into the world on your own with confidence. You can and will make it as you master living on your own for the first time!

If you have suggestions which you believe would be good additions to the guide, feel free to email me for the next edition to onyourown101@gmail.com.

Disclaimer

The contents in this book are as accurate as possible but no one can give you a complete assurance any technique or suggestion described in this book will work in each situation. While the techniques described in the book have been used with success by many, there is no guarantee you will have the same level of results.

About Chris Kelly

Chris Kelly is a mother, entrepreneur, author, certified life coach and motivational guide. She is passionate about helping people realize their dreams by stepping out of the box. In her world this is no "can't", there is only will or won't. Chris shares her experiences and motivation with clients as she helps guide them through the process of what is possible.

Chris has created multiple successful businesses, she has helped others attract to their lives things they only thought could be a dream. She leads her life as an example of how anything is possible and manifesting dreams to live a life without regrets. Chris allows no limits or boundaries to determine her destiny whether it be age, gender or geographic location.

Chris is an idea factory who passionately wants to see her clients' blossom and do what it takes to get over the excuses taking quantum leaps. Bottom line is…Chris Kelly gets things done. If you want to learn how to get things done and live your life now, Chris will put on her steel-toed stilettos, kick you in the booty and help you transform from a cocoon to a colorful butterfly with expansive wings soaring to great new heights. Chris loves life, her children, travel, beautiful beaches, searching for treasures and watching others realize their dreams and destiny passionately.

If you are ready to live life fully instead of idling and watching the time fly by, contact Chris Kelly: chriskellyink@gmail.com.

Chris is available for motivational seminars, workshops and personal coaching. She also has at home study programs to help you learn how to change your mindset, attract what you want and manifest true happiness.

Don't waste another minute being stuck.

45216458R00074

Made in the USA
Middletown, DE
28 June 2017